This Journal Belongs To:

Printed in Great Britain
by Amazon

66972409R00058